CHRISTLIKENESS
COMMITTING OURSELVES TO BE CHANGED BY GOD

FOUNDATIONS FOR
CHRISTIAN LIVING
SERIES

NAVPRESS
BRINGING TRUTH TO LIFE
NavPress Publishing Group
P.O. Box 35001, Colorado Springs, Colorado 80935

The Navigators is an international Christian organization. Our mission is to reach, disciple, and equip people to know Christ and to make Him known through successive generations. We envision multitudes of diverse people in the United States and every other nation who have a passionate love for Christ, live a lifestyle of sharing Christ's love, and multiply spiritual laborers among those without Christ.

NavPress is the publishing ministry of The Navigators. NavPress publications help believers learn biblical truth and apply what they learn to their lives and ministries. Our mission is to stimulate spiritual formation among our readers.

© 1997 by The Navigators
All rights reserved. No part of this publication may be reproduced in any form without written permission from NavPress, P.O. Box 35001, Colorado Springs, CO 80935.
ISBN 1-57683-006-3

Cover Photo by Cover Images, © 1997 Photo Disc, Inc.

The FOUNDATIONS FOR CHRISTIAN LIVING (FCL) series grew out of The Navigators' worldwide Scriptural Roots of the Ministry (SRM) process. The eight guides in this series reflect the major themes that emerged from ten years of Scriptural study, international dialogue, and prayer. It is the desire of the SRM team that those who follow Jesus Christ be grounded in these fundamental elements of the faith. For more information regarding the SRM process, please write to NavPress at the above address. The FCL series was researched and developed by Don Bartel, John Purvis, and Chuck Steen. The series text was written by Joanne Heim.

Unless otherwise identified, all Scripture quotations in this publication are taken from the *HOLY BIBLE: NEW INTERNATIONAL VERSION* ® (NIV®). Copyright © 1973, 1978, 1984 by International Bible Society, used by permission of Zondervan Publishing House, all rights reserved. The other version used is *The Message* (MSG) by Eugene H. Peterson, copyright © 1993, 1994, 1995, 1996, used by permission of NavPress Publishing Group.

Printed in the United States of America

1 2 3 4 5 6 7 8 9 10 11 12 13 14 15 / 02 01 00 99 98 97

CONTENTS

HOW TO USE THIS GUIDE

For those God foreknew he also predestined to be
conformed to the likeness of his Son. . . .

—*Romans 8:29*

When the Holy Spirit enters our lives, He embarks on a process of transforming us into persons who think, feel, and act like Christ. Many of us have misconceptions about how the process works, and consequently, we aren't sure how best to cooperate with it. What is our job, and what is God's? How does repentance work? What purposes do spiritual disciplines serve? What role does suffering play in the process, and how can other people participate? This study will help you answer these questions and more.

The FOUNDATIONS Process

The FOUNDATIONS series will help you not merely learn about God but also grow in your love for Him. Through the FOUNDATIONS process you'll grow in discovering God, experiencing one another, and serving in the world. Your group will . . .

> ▶ pursue the mystery of God together and discover ways to draw closer to Him
> ▶ grow as you learn to be honest and vulnerable with one another, deeply accepting one another
> ▶ become courageous in helping one another at the point of personal need
> ▶ discover how to live genuinely in this fast-paced, complex world
> ▶ design ways to serve God together, as a group

The nine sessions in this study follow a three-stage process:

1. Session 1 introduces you to the FOUNDATIONS series. You'll explore three essential elements of the spiritual life on which the series focuses. You'll also begin to develop relationships with the other people in your small group. Session 1 is the same in all FOUNDATIONS studies. If you have recently used another FOUNDATIONS study with your current group, you may simply review session 1 of this study.
2. Sessions 2 through 7 lead you through a variety of issues related to taking on the character of Christ.
3. Sessions 8 and 9 enable you to take stock of what you've studied and consider what you want to do about it. In session 8 you'll discern how the material applies to you as an individual. Your group will offer feedback and support in following through. In session 9 you'll discuss how the material applies to you as a group. Most of the Bible was written to groups of people rather than to individuals, so session 9 may bring your study alive in ways you did not expect. Session 9 will also help you assess your group's progress in becoming a community as you look at unity, intimacy, interdependence, and mission.

A Modular Approach

Each session is divided into four modules or sections.

OVERVIEW

The overview section briefly describes where the session is headed and what your goals will be. The key issue is stated in the paragraph labeled "So, what's the big deal?" This issue will normally be a point of tension between what the Bible teaches and what we commonly experience. The session will then help your group wrestle through that tension together.

Stating the key issue up front risks preempting the Holy Spirit from guiding your group in the direction He wants to take it, but if you remain open to His leading throughout your individual preparation and group meeting, we believe He'll use the material to minister to you in ways you wouldn't have imagined.

ON YOUR OWN   (30-60 minutes)

This section includes the passages you should be sure to examine before your group meets. You'll find some questions easy; others will stretch you mentally. We've found that a spiritual person is defined more by the internal questions he or she is asking than by the conclusions he or she has already reached. Mind-stretching questions are ideal for group discussion—be prepared for a lively debate! (And don't overlook the **For Further Study** questions, where we've hidden some of the best material in each session!)

As you work through this material, it will be helpful to remember a few "principles of understanding" that relate to learning about God:

▶ Understanding comes through mental exertion (Proverbs 2:3-5). Make sure you schedule enough preparation time to delve into the topic.

▶ Understanding comes through the soul and spirit (John 4:24). Seek God in your spirit as you study, as well as when you discuss.

▶ Understanding comes through the insight of others (Romans 1:12; Acts 17:11). Ask God to make you discerning so you will hear what He is saying to you through each other.

GROUP DISCOVERY   (40-90 minutes)

This will be the discussion portion of your group meeting. It will usually include three sub-sections:

Let's Warm Up: Each group session opens with a question or two to help you learn about each other. The warm-up questions also help you move from what you were thinking about (or worried about) when you arrived at the meeting to what the biblical texts deal with. These questions put you in touch with the topic in an experiential way, so your discussion is not just sharing ideas but sharing life. The questions in this section focus on life experiences and are usually fun to answer.

Let's Talk: In this section you'll examine one or two key Bible passages on the topic and discuss what light these passages shed on the central tension of the study. You'll also discuss any questions raised by your individual study. Feel free to bring to the group anything that perplexed or excited you in your individual study.

Let's Act: The questions in this section connect what you've studied to how you live. They often ask you to consider applying what you've learned to your group as a whole, rather than just to your individual life. Application is the reason for Bible study; be sure you allow plenty of time for it.

GROUP WORSHIP   (15-30 minutes)

In order to stress the importance of the worship portion of your meeting, we have set it apart as a special section. Worship and prayer as a group are essential components of the FOUNDATIONS process. Praying and worshiping together can be one of the most faith-building and relationship-building activities you do together. Since many people have never prayed aloud with others before, the suggestions for worship begin gently. Later in the study you'll have an opportunity to plan your own worship times. You may decide to assign one person in the group to plan and lead worship, or you may rotate the responsibility.

In session 4 you'll begin to set aside at least 15 minutes of your worship time to discuss prayerfully and humbly a question often overlooked in Bible studies: "What is the Holy Spirit saying to us?" (This is referred to as *Let's Listen to God.*) You may find it challenging to get past what you imagine God ought to be saying to the group. The experience of trying to discern God's voice will invariably draw your group to a deeper level of intimacy.

Facilitator's Job Description

Leadership is essential to an effective group. FOUNDATIONS studies will go much better if someone in your group takes responsibility to:

1. Launch the group
   ▶ Recruit people for the group, explaining its purpose and process.
   ▶ Schedule meetings (with group consensus).

8

2. Pray regularly
   - ▶ For the individual members in their daily lives.
   - ▶ For the group's growth into community.
   - ▶ For the courage and faith of the group to take the steps it needs to grow in Christ.

3. Build community
   - ▶ Stay in touch with the members, encouraging them to also stay in touch with each other.
   - ▶ Make sure that each member grows in his or her ownership of this group. (This can be done by assigning responsibility—those with responsibility usually experience ownership and genuine membership in a group.)
   - ▶ Help the group move beyond studying to doing.
   - ▶ Maintain momentum and remotivate group members if enthusiasm diminishes.

4. Facilitate rather than lead
   - ▶ Search for vision and direction together, rather than announcing vision and answers. Help the group arrive at its vision and answers. Help people go where the Spirit is leading them, rather than where you think they should go. Remind them that understanding is only the beginning; implementing is the goal.
   - ▶ Teach by asking questions, rather than making authoritative statements. Questions can often accomplish what statements cannot. Questions were Jesus' preferred style.
   - ▶ Draw out the quiet or introverted persons.
   - ▶ Encourage everyone's participation; affirm the different contributions of all.

5. Be content with less than ideal progress
   - ▶ Put up with some ambiguity. People never grow in a constant or straight line. Two steps forward and one step back is the norm. Remember what Christ has tolerated in you. Be happy with progress in the general direction of FOUNDATIONS goals.

6. Watch the clock
   - ▶ When the allotted time for a given section is over, go on to the

9

next section even if the group has not exhausted its discussion. (It is likely you will need to do this—many of the **Let's Talk** sections have more than enough material to fill the recommended time slot.) Unless you have unlimited time, the group will appreciate being kept on schedule. Don't allow discussion to consume all of your time so that application and worship must be omitted. On the other hand, if you sense the Spirit of God is actively at work, follow the Spirit's leading, not the clock. Look for an appropriate time at which to say, "I sense that God is doing something important here. Is it okay with all of you if we extend our time in this section of the meeting?"

7. Delegate
   ▶ After the first two or three sessions, ask someone else in the group to lead the worship time. Someone in your group is probably gifted in the area of worship and interested in helping the group focus on God through worship. Also, ask someone to lead the Group Discovery discussion. Direct that person to read item 4 in this job description. You could rotate this job around the group. Finally, appoint someone else to be timekeeper. By delegating these three functions, you will encourage all participants to feel like owners of the group rather than spectators.

8. Establish ground rules
   ▶ It is important that everyone in the group has a chance to buy into the rules by which the group will run. Ground rules clarify what the group expects from each person. The most important ground rules are stated on pages 17-18. Be sure to discuss them in your first meeting.

1.
THREE BIG IDEAS

OVERVIEW

In this introductory session you'll examine the three essential elements of the spiritual life on which the FOUNDATIONS series focuses: worship, community, and service. Your goals will be:

▶ To understand and own these three elements—worship, community, and service
▶ To get to know each other by telling a little of your stories and why you've joined this group

Session 1 is the same in all FOUNDATIONS studies. If you have recently used another FOUNDATIONS study with your current group, you may choose to do session 1 or merely to review it and then skip to session 2.

ON YOUR OWN (30-60 minutes)

Most of us would like to love and be loved better than we already do and are. The FOUNDATIONS series revolves around three fundamental commands Jesus gave to His followers:

▶ Love God with all your heart, soul, mind, and strength (see Mark 12:30).
▶ Love one another as Jesus loves you (see John 13:34).
▶ Love your neighbor as yourself (see Mark 12:31).

In these verses, Jesus states the "big picture" of what the spiritual life is about. We love Him through worship, we love one another through

11

community, and we love others through service. We can depict this
threefold lifestyle with the following set of concentric circles:

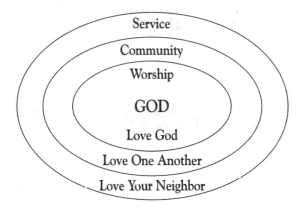

These three commands may be summarized in a single goal for the series:

*To help you become a community—a small, closely knit group moti-
vated and empowered to worship and serve God together.*

Worship, community, and service form the structural backbone of
the FOUNDATIONS process. They will direct your love toward God,
toward the others in your group, and toward your neighbors (others not
yet a part of your group). At the end of this study, you'll have a chance
to summarize what you've learned about worship, community, and service, and to assess your progress as a group toward these three
outcomes.

WORSHIP
God's commands about love show that He is vitally interested in relationships and that our relationship with Him should be our highest
priority. Worship is the all-consuming, ongoing activity of heaven. We
have the inexpressible privilege of joining in the cosmic worship of the
King already taking place in the heavenly realm.
When we see God as He is and worship Him, the other areas of
our lives begin to work themselves out. Drawing near to God's heart in
spirit and truth will inevitably affect our relationships with others.

Hence, worship will become the centerpiece of your group experience. This concentration on God will set your little community apart from a mere discussion group or gathering of friends. While early sessions of this study will include suggestions for worship, feel free to use your entire group's creativity and experience under the leadership of the Holy Spirit as you come into God's presence session by session.

The essence of worship is turning our attention toward God, reflecting His glorious attributes back to Him, and agreeing with who He is and what He has done. God delights to reveal Himself more fully to us as we worship, to satisfy our hearts' desire for relationship with Him, and to give us help for our desperate needs.

God invites us to come to Him with our burdens, needs, joys, and heartaches. In reality, we cannot come to God without our burdens; they are part of who we are. Instead of denying the things on our hearts, we'll find it far more helpful to acknowledge them as fully as possible, commit them to God, then seek Him in His greatness for who He is.

1. When you think of worship, what ideas or images come to mind?
   □ lively music
   □ majestic hymns or choral works
   □ silence and solitude
   □ lengthy sermons
   □ performers and spectators
   □ communing with nature in the woods or by a stream
   □ all of life
   □ other:

2. On a scale of 1 to 10, how would you rate your most recent experience of worship in terms of how well it focused your heart on God's greatness? Why?

1	2	3	4	5	6	7	8	9	10
dry				okay					awesome

3. Does the idea of worship being the centerpiece of your group experience attract or trouble you? Why?

COMMUNITY

From a centered place of loving God, you'll move outward to loving the others in your group. This shared life is what the New Testament writers mean by *koinonia*: "fellowship," "communion," "partnership," "participation," "community."

> We saw it, we heard it, and now we're telling you so you can experience it along with us, this experience of communion with the Father and his Son, Jesus Christ. Our motive for writing is simply this: We want you to enjoy this, too. Your joy will double our joy! (1 John 1:3-4, MSG)

In the FOUNDATIONS series we assume that dynamic Christian community as described in the New Testament is not only possible but normative for us. When we fail to experience such relationships, we miss the fullness of life that God intends for us. While there are many spiritually important things one can and should do alone, an effective community contributes equally crucial ingredients of life. People in community can:

▶ encourage one another in good times and bad
▶ ask thoughtful questions when a member has a decision to make
▶ listen to God together
▶ learn how to pray together and for one another
▶ benefit from one another's insights into Scripture
▶ acquire a habit of reading the Bible
▶ practice loving their neighbors
▶ worship God together
▶ learn to communicate effectively and solve problems together
▶ learn to receive care from others
▶ experience the pleasure of helping another person grow

Community in these studies refers to a small group of 3 to 13 people who relate in a certain way. Community in this sense is very different from any organizational form or structure. Matthew 18:20 says, "For where there are two or three who have been joined together into my Name with the result that I am the common object of their faith, there I am in their midst."[1] The individuals together are seeking intimacy with God and fellowship with each other. *Koinonia* includes partnership, participation, and contribution. It implies communication and vulnerability. It is much more than just getting together and discussing some nonvolatile topic.

Jesus wanted His disciples to experience a unique relationship when they came together—unique in their love for and their unity with one another. When genuine love is present, a group has taken the first and biggest step toward real community. This process is not easy. Your group will probably have to resolve a number of relational issues on the road to biblical community.

4. What appeals to you about this description of community?

5. What questions or concerns do you have about this kind of community? Explain.

SERVICE

Any community focused on God loves to serve both believers and unbelievers, just as God does. How could it be otherwise? You'll find that as your group grows in worshiping God and loving one another, the members will intuitively know they need to be helping others. This will be natural.

What may not be natural is serving together as a team and serving the lost—both of which Jesus did and which His followers throughout history have done.

Most of us slowly abandon former friends and acquaintances when we join the kingdom of God. We're not comfortable anymore around those who do not share our new values. Our old friends no longer feel comfortable around us. Somehow we lose the ability Jesus had to be "a friend of tax collectors and 'sinners'" (Matthew 11:19). It is far easier for us to serve those within the kingdom of God than those more distant.

And if somehow we do seek to draw the lost toward Christ, we usually do so as individuals, rather than in partnership with other believers. Consequently, those who need the Savior never experience the powerful influence of a loving community.

The FOUNDATIONS studies will guide your group into these two dimensions: serving the lost and serving together. Serving does not exclusively mean explaining the gospel verbally. Loving our neighbor often translates into specific acts of compassionate service at home, neighborhood, or work. We often serve individually, but this FOUNDATIONS guide will focus your efforts on serving God's interests together. You will not be told what to do; you will not be pushed beyond your point of willing consent. Rather, you will decide together how to put what you are studying into practice outside your group.

6. What thoughts and feelings does this description of service raise for you?
   ☐ Excitement—I'm ready to go!
   ☐ Discomfort—The last thing I need is more on my "to-do" list.
   ☐ Anxiety—I did door-to-door witnessing several years ago and hated it. Will we have to do that again?
   ☐ Ambivalence—I have a strong desire to serve more, but I know it's not easy for me.
   ☐ Confusion—Isn't it good enough for us just to take care of each other for awhile?
   ☐ Relief—I'm glad this isn't just another navel-gazing group.
   ☐ Other (explain):

7. Is this statement true of you: "It is far easier for us to serve those within the kingdom of God than those more distant." If so, why do you think that is?

8. We have stated three priorities: loving God, loving others in the group, and loving others outside the group. What about loving yourself? Do you think this should be a priority ahead of any or all of these three? Explain your view.

 GROUP DISCOVERY (40-90 minutes)

Let's Warm Up (10 minutes)

Beginning with the leader, let each person take one minute to answer question 9.

9. Recall an important friendship from your childhood. Who was that friend, and what was special about that friendship? What bond kept you and that friend together?

Let's Talk (30 minutes)

10. Share your responses to questions 1-8 in the "On Your Own" section. Discuss any questions you have about the three big ideas stated there.

11. Discuss the following ground rules for your group. Feel free to change anything. The objective is for everyone to be content with the result, not for everyone to go along while harboring private reservations.

☐ Purpose: The reason our group exists is to become a community—a small, closely knit group motivated and empowered to worship and serve God.

☐ Participation: I am committed to participating in this community, to worshiping, and to serving others outside the group.

☐ Attendance: I will be here as often as possible. This group will be a priority.

☐ Ownership: I agree to share responsibility for our group goals.

☐ Confidentiality: I agree to keep here whatever is shared here.

☐ Accountability: I agree to give permission to the other group members to hold me accountable for goals I set for myself.

☐ Accessibility: I give group members permission to call me when they are in need—even in the middle of the night. My phone number is. . . .

GROUP WORSHIP (15-30 minutes)

12. Pray that God would begin to reveal Himself in more of His majesty, power, and direction.

13. Read aloud together this portion of Psalm 89 (from *The Message*):

Your love, GOD, is my song, and I'll sing it!
    I'm forever telling everyone how faithful you are.
I'll never quit telling the story of your love—
    how you built the cosmos
    and guaranteed everything in it.
Your love has always been our lives' foundation,
    your fidelity has been the roof over our world.
You once said, "I joined forces with my chosen leader,
    I pledged my word to my servant, David, saying,
'Everyone descending from you is guaranteed life;
    I'll make your rule as solid and lasting as rock.'"

GOD! Let the cosmos praise your wonderful ways,
    the choir of holy angels sing anthems to your faithful ways!
Search high and low, scan skies and land,
    you'll find nothing and no one quite like GOD.
The holy angels are in awe before him;
    he looms immense and august over everyone around him.
GOD of the Angel Armies, who is like you,
    powerful and faithful from every angle?
You put the arrogant ocean in its place
    and calm its waves when they turn unruly.

You gave that old hag Egypt the back of your hand,
    you brushed off your enemies with a flick of your wrist.
You own the cosmos—you made everything in it,
    everything from atom to archangel.
You positioned the North and South Poles;
    the mountains Tabor and Hermon sing duets to you.
With your well-muscled arm and your grip of steel—
    nobody trifles with you!
The Right and Justice are the roots of your rule;
    Love and Truth are its fruits.
Blessed are the people who know the passwords of praise,
    who shout on parade in the bright presence of GOD.
Delighted, they dance all day long; they know
    who you are, what you do—they can't keep it quiet!
Your vibrant beauty has gotten inside us—
    you've been so good to us! We're walking on air!
All we are and have we owe to GOD,
    Holy God of Israel, our King! (Psalm 89:1-18, MSG)

14. Allow a moment of silence for everyone to focus on God. In worship, you have no agenda but to focus on Him.

15. Beginning with the leader, let each person thank God for one thing he or she learned in this session, or praise God for one aspect of Himself highlighted in your discussion. If you are comfortable doing so, allow for additional, spontaneous expressions of thanks and praise.

Optional

If you think your group might appreciate singing together, ask someone to lead with guitar or other instrument. If no one in your group has that skill, consider singing with a CD; some are now designed especially for small group worship. Be sure the person who leads worship understands that singing is only one aspect of worship, and that he or she should limit singing to the time allotted in your schedule.

---

1. Wuest, Kenneth S. *The New Testament: An Expanded Translation.* Grand Rapids, Mich.: Eerdmans, 1961.

2.

THE HOLY SPIRIT'S ROLE IN PRODUCING CHRISTLIKENESS

*And we, who with unveiled faces all reflect the
Lord's glory, are being transformed into his likeness
with ever-increasing glory, which comes from the Lord,
who is the Spirit.*

—2 Corinthians 3:18

OVERVIEW

To believe in Jesus Christ is to begin a process of
becoming like Christ. The apostle Paul writes, "For those God
foreknew he also predestined to be conformed to the likeness of his
Son" (Romans 8:29). There are several ways to go about this process of
transformation. One is the white-knuckle approach. We try very hard
to act like Jesus as often as possible. We engage in as much religious
activity as possible, perhaps teaching Sunday school, attending Bible
studies, and spending lots of time praying and reading the Bible.

A second strategy is the mellow approach. We go about our business as usual, waiting for the Holy Spirit to change us into something
entirely different.

In this session, you'll evaluate these two strategies in light of two
passages from the letters of Paul. Your goal will be to decide what it
means to take off the old self and put on the new one, and what it
means to live by the Spirit. Your central focus will be on the Holy
Spirit's role in the change process.

So, what's the big deal?
If we misunderstand the Spirit's role in our transformation, we face two

risks: becoming legalistic or effort oriented, which can lead to burnout and frustration, or spending our whole Christian lives in spiritual babyhood.

ON YOUR OWN (30-60 minutes)

The Greek word for transformation is *metamorphosis*. It describes a change in form or character of a substance's innate nature. For example, a caterpillar's form is completely changed when it turns into a butterfly.

1. What pictures come to mind when you think of yourself transformed to be like Christ?

When the apostle Paul talks to the Ephesians about transformation into the likeness of Christ, he uses the imagery of a person taking off one set of clothes and putting on a new set. However, the change he envisions is much more than external.

> So I tell you this, and insist on it in the Lord, that you must no longer live as the Gentiles do, in the futility of their thinking. They are darkened in their understanding and separated from the life of God because of the ignorance that is in them due to the hardening of their hearts. Having lost all sensitivity, they have given themselves over to sensuality so as to indulge in every kind of impurity, with a continual lust for more.
> You, however, did not come to know Christ that way. Surely you heard of him and were taught in him in accordance with the truth that is in Jesus. You were taught, with regard to your former way of life, to put off your old self, which is being corrupted by its deceitful desires; to be made new in the attitude of your minds;

and to put on the new self, created to be like God in true righteousness and holiness. (Ephesians 4:17-24)

2. How does Paul describe the old self? What are its traits?

3. What do you think Paul means when he says to put off your old self?

4. a. What are some of the things connected with the old self (attitudes, deceitful desires, et cetera) that you find the hardest to let go of?

   b. What makes them difficult to leave?

5. Paul talks about being "made new in the attitude of your minds." What do you think that means?

6. How are attitudes related to behaviors?

7. Paul goes on to give his readers numerous examples of what the new life looks like in contrast to the old. After you read the passage below, list the values, feelings, and behaviors that Paul tells us to change.

> Therefore each of you must put off falsehood and speak truthfully to his neighbor, for we are all members of one body. "In your anger do not sin": Do not let the sun go down while you are still angry, and do not give the devil a foothold. He who has been stealing must steal no longer, but must work, doing something useful with his own hands, that he may have something to share with those in need.
>
> Do not let any unwholesome talk come out of your mouths, but only what is helpful for building others up according to their needs, that it may benefit those who listen. And do not grieve the Holy Spirit of God, with whom you were sealed for the day of redemption. Get rid of all bitterness, rage and anger, brawling and slander, along with every form of malice. Be kind and compassionate to one another, forgiving each other, just as in Christ God forgave you. (Ephesians 4:25-32)

☐ Values to change

☐ Feelings to change

☐ Behaviors to change

8. What would have to change in you for you to be angry without sinning, to say only things that build others up, and to be routinely compassionate?

9. How does this kind of change happen? What do you think needs to happen for change of this kind to take place?

On its own, this passage may give the impression that putting off the old and putting on the new is a matter of sheer willpower. However, the passage follows an earlier one in which Paul prays for his readers. The prayer begins with "For this reason," so it's helpful to go back to what "this reason" is and read the entire passage in context. (We've omitted 3:1-13, in which Paul starts to say "For this reason" and then digresses momentarily. We've also omitted several verses in chapter 2 for the same reason. You may find it helpful to read all of chapters 2 and 3 to get the full context of Paul's prayer.)

For through him we both have access to the Father by one Spirit.

And in him you too are being built together to become a dwelling in which God lives by his Spirit.

For this reason I kneel before the Father, from whom his whole family in heaven and on earth derives its name. I pray that out of his glorious riches he may strengthen you with power through his Spirit in your inner being, so that Christ may dwell in your hearts through faith. And I pray that you, being rooted and established in love, may have power, together with all the saints, to grasp how wide and long and high and deep is the love of Christ, and to know this love that surpasses knowledge—that you may be filled to the measure of all the fullness of God.

Now to him who is able to do immeasurably more than all we ask or imagine, according to his power that is at work within us, to him be glory in the church and in Christ Jesus throughout all generations, for ever and ever! Amen. (Ephesians 2:18,22; 3:14-21)

10. According to these excerpts from Ephesians 2–3, what role does the Spirit play in the putting off of the old self and the putting on of the new? List what the Spirit does for us.

GROUP DISCOVERY   (50-90 minutes)

Let's Warm Up (10 minutes)

11. If you could be changed into another person for a day, who would you become and why?

Let's Talk (30-50 minutes)

12. Discuss the "On Your Own" questions. What did you learn about the old and new selves? About the Spirit? About yourself?

Part of putting on the new self that Paul describes in Ephesians is learning to live by the Spirit. But what does that really mean?

The Galatians struggled with that very question. In their efforts to grow in Christ, they had caved in to living by the Jewish ritual law (circumcision, food restrictions, and so on). Some teachers had told them that living by a system of religious do's and don'ts was the only alternative to living by their lowest impulses. In this passage, Paul speaks of a third way: living by the Spirit.

> You, my brothers, were called to be free. But do not use your freedom to indulge the sinful nature; rather, serve one another in love. The entire law is summed up in a single command: "Love your neighbor as yourself." If you keep on biting and devouring each other, watch out or you will be destroyed by each other.
>
> So I say, live by the Spirit, and you will not gratify the desires of the sinful nature. For the sinful nature desires what is contrary to the Spirit, and the Spirit what is contrary to the sinful nature. They are in conflict with each other, so that you do not do what you want. But if you are led by the Spirit, you are not under law.
>
> The acts of the sinful nature are obvious: sexual immorality, impurity and debauchery; idolatry and witchcraft; hatred, discord, jealousy, fits of rage, selfish ambition, dissensions, factions and envy; drunkenness, orgies, and the like. I warn you, as I did before, that those who live like this will not inherit the kingdom of God.
>
> But the fruit of the Spirit is love, joy, peace, patience, kindness, goodness, faithfulness, gentleness and self-control. Against such things there is no law. Those who belong to Christ Jesus have crucified the sinful nature with its passions and desires. Since we live by the Spirit, let us keep in step with the Spirit.
> (Galatians 5:13-25)

13. What do you think Paul means when he tells us to live by the Spirit?

14. Read the following story together, then answer the questions that follow.

Travis has an extensive spiritual "to do" list. Each day he gets up early and spends at least an hour reading his Bible and praying. He's a member of a men's group that meets for breakfast once a week, and he attends a couples' Bible study on Thursday nights with his wife. He participates in church leadership and teaches Sunday school.

Travis wants to become more like Christ but feels like he has hit the wall. Although he is frustrated and feels like a failure for not being mature enough in Christ, he doesn't have the capacity to add any more to his plate. Despite his rigorous efforts to grow spiritually, he often snaps at his kids and shows impatience with his wife. He gets angry easily and has a hard time accepting other people's failures.

☐ Would you say Travis is living by the Spirit?

☐ If you were Travis' spiritual doctor, what would you prescribe for his spiritual health?

15. Living by the Spirit can seem vague. In Romans 8:5, Paul elaborates:

> Those who live according to the sinful nature have their minds set on what that nature desires; but those who live in accordance with the Spirit have their minds set on what the Spirit desires.

What do you think it looks like for a person to set his or her mind on what the Spirit desires?

16. What's hard about setting one's mind on what the Spirit desires and living by the Spirit's direction?

☐ I have always thought that disciplines like Scripture memory, church attendance and prayer are what draws me closer to God. If I let the Spirit take over, what is it that I am supposed to be doing?

☐ My head is full of what I desire. It's very hard for me to think about anything else.

☐ I'd like to experience the kind of freedom Paul talks about, but I'm afraid of the way the Spirit might work in my life. At least with my own efforts, I know what to expect.

☐ I'm not clear on what the Spirit desires or does.

☐ I don't know how to recognize the difference between the Spirit's promptings and my own desires.

☐ Other (please explain):

17. What do you think would happen if you lived by the Spirit? How would your life be different?

18. What would you say to someone who . . .

☐ feels a disciplined approach to the Christian life will bring about Christlikeness?

☐ believes the Spirit accomplishes His work automatically without any effort on the part of the believer?

Let's Act (15-30 minutes)

19. As a result of your discussion, what might the Holy Spirit be communicating to your group about becoming like Christ? (Think about the Holy Spirit's message to you as a group, rather than to each of you as individuals.)

20. How could this group help you live by the Spirit?

21. How does what you have discussed in this session affect these things?

    ☐ Your worship

    ☐ Your relationships as a group

    ☐ Your responsibilities/relationships with others (neighbors, coworkers, family, seekers, new believers, disciples, enemies, et cetera)

GROUP WORSHIP   (15-30 minutes)

22. Begin your time of worship by reading the following psalm as a group.

Hallelujah!

Thank God! Pray to him by name!
    Tell everyone you meet what he has done!
Sing him songs, belt out hymns,
    translate his wonders into music!
Honor his holy name with Hallelujahs,
    you who seek God. Live a happy life!
Keep your eyes open for God, watch for his works;
    be alert for signs of his presence. (Psalm 105:1-4, MSG)

23. If your group is so inclined, sing a chorus or a hymn as you meditate and pray.

24. Spend some time in prayer thanking God for His desire to transform you into the image of His Son. Praise Him that He uses the Holy Spirit to accomplish this purpose and that spiritual maturity isn't something you have to achieve on your own. Pray that you would turn to Him for help in those areas you find most difficult to change.

3.
THE PLACE OF REPENTANCE IN BECOMING LIKE CHRIST

Godly sorrow brings repentance that leads to salvation
and leaves no regret, but worldly sorrow brings death.
                                        —2 Corinthians 7:10

OVERVIEW

Remember getting caught with your hand in the cookie jar when you were little? It was easy to feel sorry for being caught but a little harder to be sorry for disobeying mom. As adults, we still have a hard time dealing with our sin. Somehow, the most embarrassing and difficult thing is not what we did wrong, but that other people know we did it.

The godly sorrow that Paul describes in 2 Corinthians plays a big role in our transformation. Repentance leads to lasting change and restoration with God and others, while remorse usually means being sorry only that we were caught.

In this session, we will learn the difference between repentance and remorse, and examine the responses of the lost son, Peter, and Judas to their sin. Your goal will be to understand the nature of true repentance and godly sorrow, as well as how God uses repentance to transform you into Christ's image.

So, what's the big deal?
It's easy to work up feelings of remorse, but they don't make us more like Christ. Genuine repentance changes us, but we can't manufacture it.

1. What comes to mind when you think of repentance?

☐ Getting caught doing something wrong
☐ Being sorry for hurting someone else
☐ Wishing I hadn't done anything wrong
☐ Blaming someone else for mistakes
☐ Committing to a change in behavior
☐ Weeping, wailing, and groveling
☐ Apologizing
☐ Making things right again
☐ Other (please explain):

Repentance is a change of mind and heart that produces real and lasting change. Some of the confusion surrounding repentance can be traced to translation difficulties. Latin versions of the Bible translated the Greek word *metanoia* (a change of mind or purpose) into "to exercise penitence." This way of translating suggests paying for your sin but not changing your thoughts or actions.

2. The religious leaders of Jesus' day were appalled that He welcomed and socialized with tax collectors (people who collaborated with Rome, the enemy, lining their own pockets in the process) and their equally immoral friends. In response to their criticism, Jesus told three parables about God's response to people who have lost their way (Luke 15). Luke 15:11-32 is the third and longest of the three, and it presents a vivid picture of repentance. Read this story, and list the characteristics of the younger son's life before and after repentance.

3. Why did the younger son repent of his sin?

4. How does the text describe the moment of his repentance?

5. How would you have felt if you were the younger son approaching his father?
   - ☐ Scared. My father has already given me my inheritance and doesn't owe me anything more.
   - ☐ Hopeful. I hope my father will understand.
   - ☐ Hesitant. My father might understand, but I can't be sure.
   - ☐ Ashamed. I've sunk to the bottom of the barrel and know I'm not worthy to be called my father's child.
   - ☐ Confident. I know my father loves me and will take me back.
   - ☐ Other (please explain):

6. What evidence, if any, do you see in the story of a change in the younger son's character? Do you think he really repented of his sin, or was he just sorry about the way things turned out?

7. The older son was unhappy with the forgiveness his brother received. Why do you think he responded the way he did?

8. Which character in the story do you relate to the most? Why?

9. What does it usually take for you to "come to your senses" and repent?

10. What do your answers to questions 4-9 teach you about repentance?

The apostle Paul had quite a time moving the feisty group of believers in Corinth to genuine repentance. First Corinthians contains Paul's rebuke for several major problems, especially factional fighting and arrogance of the strong toward the weak. Some of the people he rebuked refused to listen to him, even when he later came in person. He called that visit "painful" (2 Corinthians 2:1) because one or more of the Corinthians evidently challenged his authority. He then sent a "tearful" letter (2 Corinthians 2:4) that is now lost to us. That letter apparently hit home. In the following passage from 2 Corinthians, which he wrote after receiving news that the tearful letter had worked, Paul describes the kind of repentance he had been looking for.

> Even if I caused you sorrow by my letter, I do not regret it. Though I did regret it —I see that my letter hurt you, but only for a little while—yet now I am happy, not because you were made sorry, but because your sorrow led you to repentance. For you became sorrowful as God intended and so were not harmed in any way by us. Godly sorrow brings repentance that leads to salvation and leaves no regret, but worldly sorrow brings death. See what

this godly sorrow has produced in you: what earnestness, what eagerness to clear yourselves, what indignation, what alarm, what longing, what concern, what readiness to see justice done. At every point you have proved yourselves to be innocent in this matter. (2 Corinthians 7:8-11)

11. How does Paul describe true repentance?

12. What do you think he means by godly sorrow? How is it different from worldly sorrow?

13. Paul says godly sorrow leaves no regret. Have you ever experienced sorrow without regret? If so, describe it.

14. Is there anything in your life right now about which you need to repent?

For Additional Study

As you think about repentance, read each of the following passages and answer these three questions:

☐ What is the starting point for repentance?
☐ How does repentance occur?
☐ What are the evidences of true repentance?

▶ Luke 3:3,7-20   ▶ James 1:19-25
▶ John 16:7-11   ▶ 1 John 1:5–2:6
▶ 2 Corinthians 7:8-12

 GROUP DISCOVERY   (50-90 minutes)

Let's Warm Up (10 minutes)

15. Describe a time from your childhood when you were caught doing something wrong. What did you do when you were caught?

Let's Talk (30-50 minutes)

16. Discuss your answers to the "On Your Own" questions. What did you learn about remorse? About repentance? About yourself?

17. What evidence do you see in society of remorse (feeling sorry for sin) and repentance (taking action to stop sin)?

18. From what you've seen, do you think believers deal with remorse and repentance differently than society does? Explain.

19. How does God use repentance to make us more like Christ?

20. On the night when Jesus was betrayed by Judas and arrested, He predicted that Peter would deny Him three times. Peter was aghast at the thought and swore it would never happen. Matthew 26:69–27:5 describes how Peter and Judas responded when they realized their sin. Read the passage aloud.

   a. How were Peter's and Judas's responses to their sin similar?

   b. How were they different?

21. It's clear that both Peter and Judas had strong feelings of remorse when they realized their sin. Do you think Peter experienced the kind of godly sorrow Paul describes? Why do you say that?

22. What about Judas? Did he experience godly sorrow and repentance? How can you tell?

23. What can you learn from Peter and Judas about remorse and repentance?

Let's Act (15-30 minutes)

24. As a result of your discussion, what might the Holy Spirit be communicating to your group about repentance? (Think about the Holy Spirit's message to you as a group, rather than to each of you as individuals.)

25. a. Are you more prone to remorse or repentance? Explain.

    b. How can this group encourage true repentance among its members? How could the group support you in repentance?

26. How does what you've learned about repentance affect these things?

    ☐ Your worship

    ☐ Your relationships as a group

    ☐ Your responsibilities/relationships with others (neighbors, coworkers, family, seekers, new believers, disciples, enemies, et cetera).

27. As a group, read and pray through Psalm 40:1-8.

I waited patiently for the LORD;
    he turned to me and heard my cry.
He lifted me out of the slimy pit,
    out of the mud and mire;
he set my feet on a rock
    and gave me a firm place to stand.
He put a new song in my mouth,
    a hymn of praise to our God.
Many will see and fear
    and put their trust in the LORD.
Blessed is the man
    who makes the LORD his trust,
who does not look to the proud,
    to those who turn aside to false gods.
Many, O LORD my God,
    are the wonders you have done.
The things you planned for us
    no one can recount to you;
were I to speak and tell of them,
    they would be too many to declare.
Sacrifice and offering you did not desire,
    but my ears you have pierced;
burnt offerings and sin offerings
    you did not require.
Then I said, "Here I am, I have come—
    it is written about me in the scroll.
I desire to do your will, O my God;
    your law is within my heart." (Psalm 40:1-8)

28. Use this psalm as a springboard to confession of sin and/or prayer
about your own desire to do God's will. Thank God for His forgiveness. If your group is so inclined, sing an appropriate chorus or
hymn as you meditate and pray.

4.

TRANSFORMING ENCOUNTERS WITH GOD

Most of life is pretty ordinary. We go about the day-to-day business of living, vaguely aware of God's presence and His purpose of transforming us into Christ's image. But there are those defining experiences with God, where change occurs quickly and growth happens in spurts, rather than gradually.

The Bible is full of such encounters. God spoke to many people in the Old Testament, appeared to others throughout the Bible, and caused drastic change in people's lives. In this session, you'll look at the encounters Jacob, Saul, and Peter had with God and compare those with your own experiences with God. By studying these encounters, you'll learn how God works through transforming encounters and how you can be open to them.

So, what's the big deal?

The Bible is full of stories of God's dramatic encounters with His people. To modern readers, these encounters can seem strange and unattainable. Why do people have transforming encounters with God—and why don't they seem as common today?

ON YOUR OWN (30-60 minutes)

1. What comes to mind when you think of a dramatic encounter with God?

Jacob, Abraham's grandson, was a little hard headed. He preferred to do things his own way, swindling his way into whatever caught his eye. And it usually worked. But after twenty years of hard work for an uncle who was even more of a cheater than he was, Jacob needed help. His wives bickered, his cousins threatened, his servants complained, and Jacob was on the run again. Slowly, he realized that running might not be the answer. Maybe God could help.

In Genesis 32:22-32, Jacob is about to meet his brother Esau—the one he cheated out of an inheritance. He spends the night wrestling. Read Genesis 32:22-32 from your favorite translation paying special attention to how God and Jacob interacted in this encounter.

2. What was Jacob's encounter with God like? Describe what you observe.

3. How do you react to this story? What questions come to mind?

4. Why do you think God appeared to Jacob and not the rest of his family?

5. Many elements of the stories of transforming encounters from the Bible can seem curious and hard to understand. For example, why do you think the man injured Jacob's hip?

6. Jacob was bold in refusing to let the man go until he blessed Jacob. If God (or a man like this) appeared to you, would you insist upon His granting you a request before He left? If so, what would you ask for? If not, why not?

7. How was Jacob changed because of his encounter with God? (You might read Genesis 33:1-11 and 35:1-7 in addition to the passage in Genesis 32.)

8. Saul wasn't exactly Christ's friend. As a devout Jew, he expressed his devotion to God by tracking down Jesus' followers and killing them. In fact, he was so successful in Jerusalem that he decided to broaden his territory. It might seem that Saul was the last person God would want to use for His glory. But God had plans for Saul. Read Acts 9:1-19, and note Saul's character before and after his encounter with the Lord.

☐ Before

☐ After

9. What was Saul's encounter with the Lord like?

10. Saul's conversion was more dramatic than most. Why do you think Christ interacted with Saul in such a dramatic way?

11. God also spoke to Ananias. Why do you think God chose to use Ananias as part of Saul's encounter with God?

12. Saul was completely transformed because of his encounter with God. Do you think Ananias was changed, too? Explain.

13. a. These encounters were dramatic. Each was unexpected and resulted in significant change. Not everyone has encounters quite as dramatic. Less dramatic encounters could be described as conversion, rebirth, regeneration, or even times of unusual conviction about what God wanted you to do. Think back to an encounter you had with God that has affected your spiritual journey. What happened?

b. How is your life different as a result?

For Additional Study

The Bible is full of stories of people who have had dramatic, life-changing encounters with God. What patterns or themes do you see in the passages below? As you read them, pay attention to how you can learn from their experiences.

▶ Joshua 5:12-15   ▶ Luke 24:13-32
▶ 1 Samuel 1:9-20   ▶ Luke 24:36-40
▶ Job 42:1-6   ▶ Acts 8:26-38
▶ Jeremiah 1:4-19   ▶ Acts 10:9-18
▶ Luke 5:1-11

 GROUP DISCOVERY   **(50-90 minutes)**

Let's Warm Up (10 minutes)

14. If you could instantly change one thing about yourself, what would it be?

Let's Talk (30-50 minutes)

15. Discuss your answers to the "On Your Own" questions. What did you learn about how God interacts with people? About your own experience of God? What questions do the passages raise for you?

Jesus' disciples had been living on the edge for weeks. He had sent them out to talk about the kingdom of God and to demonstrate their message by healing people. At the end of their mission, Jesus had taken them off to a remote place to debrief and relax, but a crowd of five thousand people had tracked them down. Jesus had ended up teaching the crowd all day and then involved His disciples in a miracle to feed the thousands. But the crowd misunderstood His teaching about the kingdom and tried to make Him king immediately and by force. So Jesus told the disciples to make themselves scarce while He dealt with the volatile mob. Off the disciples went by boat across the Sea of Galilee, their heads still whirling. Matthew 14:22-33 tells what happened next. Read that passage aloud.

16. Describe Peter's encounter with God in this instance.

17. Why do you think Peter doubted even though he knew it was Jesus?

18. How do you think Peter was changed as a result of his experience on the lake?

19. How do you think you would respond to a dramatic encounter with God like those Jacob, Saul, and Peter experienced?
    □ I think I would know it was God and pay attention to what He wanted to tell me.
    □ I think I would want to believe but then succumb to doubt as Peter did.
    □ I think I'd die of a heart attack!
    □ Those experiences seem foreign to me. I don't even know how to think about them.
    □ I think I would assume I'd misread the situation, that it wasn't really supernatural after all.
    □ I've had encounters like this and have learned from them.
    □ Other (please explain):

20. Have you ever had a dramatic encounter with God? Describe it.

21. If you haven't, is it something you'd like to experience? Why, or why not?

22. Since God uses these encounters to transform people, do you think this is something we should pray for?

23. Why are there numerous examples of such dramatic encounters in the Bible, but we don't hear of many today?

☐ I don't think God works that way any more.

☐ I think those kinds of encounters do happen, but we discount them as fabrications when they do.

☐ I think God does work that way today, but we aren't aware of them because we're not looking for them.

☐ I think that just as many of them happen today—after all, God didn't appear to everyone who lived back then. The Bible just collects the few cases of dramatic encounters among the thousands of cases of people who never had them.

☐ I think God would do these kinds of things if we had more faith.

☐ Other (please explain):

Let's Act (15-30 minutes)

24. Has your group's experience of God been characterized mostly by routine experiences with God or dramatic encounters?

25. Do you think your group should become more open to experiencing God in dramatic ways? If so, how can you do that? If not, why?

GROUP WORSHIP   (15-30 minutes)

26. Read Psalm 1 (on the next page) out loud, pausing after every few lines to allow anyone to comment or pray about what was read.

> Blessed is the man
> > who does not walk in the counsel of the wicked
> > or stand in the way of sinners or sit in the seat of
> > > mockers.

But his delight is in the law of the LORD,
   and on his law he meditates day and night.
He is like a tree planted by streams of water,
   which yields its fruit in season
and whose leaf does not wither.
   Whatever he does prospers.
Not so the wicked!
   They are like chaff that the wind blows away.
Therefore the wicked will not stand in the judgment,
   nor sinners in the assembly of the righteous.
For the LORD watches over the way of the righteous,
   but the way of the wicked will perish. (Psalm 1:1-6)

27. If your group is so inclined, sing an appropriate chorus or hymn as
you meditate and pray.

Let's Listen to God (15 minutes)

Throughout this study guide the question, "What do you think the
Holy Spirit is saying to your group about . . . ?" is raised. Perhaps it
seems presumptuous to claim to know what the Spirit is saying.
Perhaps you are confident that you know, or maybe you are willing to
settle for what you think the Spirit *ought* to be saying to your group.

Listening to the Spirit's voice is a skill your group can develop over
time. It requires discipline and the willingness to cultivate certain attitudes and take certain risks. As you begin your time of listening to
God, read aloud the following commitments. These are not once-for-
all-time commitments; each one will require a process of commitment
and recommitment by each group member.

▶ We acknowledge our own agendas, plans, philosophies, ideas, and
paradigms, and we determine not to let them interfere with our
relationship with God or with each other. We may not get this
right all the time, but will keep it in mind every week as we meet.

▶ We commit ourselves to being open, honest, vulnerable, available, and transparent. Of course, if we're going to do this for
real, we will have to deal with the relationship tensions and

51

conflicts that arise. The result will be the beginning of authentic relationships.

▶ We present ourselves to God in humility, poverty of spirit, brokenness, contrition, and submission. God says He is near to these kinds of persons (Isaiah 57:15, 66:2). The prophet Azariah told the king and people of Judah:

> "The LORD is with you when you are with him. If you seek him, he will be found by you, but if you forsake him, he will forsake you. For a long time Israel was without the true God. . . . But in their distress they turned to the LORD, the God of Israel, and sought him, and he was found by them." (2 Chronicles 15:1-4)

Your agenda for this time of listening to God is to try to hear what God is saying through each group member as you share your thoughts on the following questions. Your challenge is to listen to God while talking to each other. Take a moment for silent prayer, then spend about fifteen minutes on the following:

28. After reading aloud the preceding three commitments, discuss what you sense the Holy Spirit is communicating to your group about the following areas.

☐ Your worship and relationship with God

☐ Your relationships with each other

☐ Your relationships with those outside this group

Take a moment to close this conversation in prayer.

5.

CHRISTIAN DISCIPLINES THAT LEAD TO FREEDOM

For God did not give us a spirit of timidity, but a spirit of power, of love and of self-discipline.

—2 *Timothy 1:7*

OVERVIEW

There's a fine line between living by your performance and living a disciplined life under grace. We are saved solely by grace, but the Bible is full of commands regarding our actions. Since transformation is the work of the Holy Spirit, to what extent do we really need to practice discipline in our faith?

In this session, you will define spiritual discipline, learn the differences between form and function in the spiritual life, examine how the early church functioned, and compare their experiences to your own. Your goal will be to decide how spiritual disciplines can be positive influences in your life, rather than negative ones.

So, what's the big deal?
If we're saved only by grace, what role does discipline play in our process of becoming like Christ?

ON YOUR OWN   (30-60 minutes)

1. What picture or feeling comes to mind when you think about discipline?

2. The dictionary describes discipline as "training that produces obedience, self-control, or a particular skill." Would you describe yourself as a disciplined person? Why, or why not?

3. Discipline is often viewed as negative. It is also defined as "punishment given to correct a person or force obedience." Many of the verses about discipline in the Bible deal with God disciplining His people for sin. How are punishment and training related?

A key to spiritual disciplines is understanding the differences between form and function. Function is most easily described as what needs to be accomplished, and form is how you accomplish that goal. For example, the function of waking up in the morning used to be accomplished in the form of a crowing rooster. Today, people still need to wake up every morning but use the form of an alarm clock to accomplish that function.

When forms are confused with functions, they can easily outlive their original purposes. When this happens, forms become distracting and restrictive. What if we all felt compelled to keep roosters because that's what worked for our grandparents? In the same way, a weekly meeting designed to pray for others can become such an arena for gossip that the original purpose is never met. In that case, the form needs to change—either back to the original form or forward to a new form—so that the original function can be met.

The book of Acts chronicles the beginning of the early church. In the passages below, Luke describes some of the practices of the church. As you read the verses, note the specific things the church did.

> They devoted themselves to the apostles' teaching and to the fellowship, to the breaking of bread and to prayer. Everyone was filled with awe, and many wonders and miraculous signs were done

by the apostles. All the believers were together and had everything in common. Selling their possessions and goods, they gave to anyone as he had need. Every day they continued to meet together in the temple courts. They broke bread in their homes and ate together with glad and sincere hearts, praising God and enjoying the favor of all the people. And the Lord added to their number daily those who were being saved. (Acts 2:42-47)

All the believers were one in heart and mind. No one claimed that any of his possessions was his own, but they shared everything they had. With great power the apostles continued to testify to the resurrection of the Lord Jesus, and much grace was upon them all. There were no needy persons among them. For from time to time those who owned lands or houses sold them, brought the money from the sales and put it at the apostles' feet, and it was distributed to anyone as he had need. (Acts 4:32-35)

4. What were some of the forms (actions) the early church practiced? What were the functions (purposes) behind those forms?

FORMS	FUNCTIONS

5. Why do you think these functions were necessary for people saved by grace?

6. a. Do you think the early church's forms are things we are required to do or only examples of the kinds of things we should do? Why do you think so?

   b. What about the functions in the early church? Explain.

7. a. Are there functions in the list that you still do today but with different forms? Which are they?

   b. Which ones do you practice in the same way?

   c. Which do you not practice at all?

8. What is one function important to becoming like Christ that you have trouble practicing consistently?

In 1 Timothy, Paul writes to a younger man whom he has mentored for years. He has sent Timothy to the city of Ephesus to root out the influence of some men who are distorting the gospel. Among other teachings, these men have been saying that all spiritual people must practice certain disciplines: lifelong celibacy and abstinence from certain foods (1 Timothy 4:3). Paul himself is celibate, but he doesn't think everyone must follow that form of sexual discipline; monogamy is an equally sound alternative (1 Corinthians 7). He has seen merit in abstinence from certain foods in some situations (Romans 14, 1 Corinthians 8-10), but he doesn't see it as a helpful law for all cases.

In 1 Timothy 4:7-8, Paul explains the purpose of practicing spiritual disciplines. Disciplines that don't serve this purpose are no more than "godless myths and old wives' tales."

Have nothing to do with godless myths and old wives' tales; rather, train yourself to be godly. For physical training is of some value, but godliness has value for all things, holding promise for both the present life and the life to come. (1 Timothy 4:7-8)

9. What is the goal of a good spiritual discipline, according to Paul?

10. What are some of the ways that you are training yourself to be godly and like Christ?

11. What would it look like for you to be completely disciplined about pursuing godliness? What would change?

For Additional Study
In the following passages, identify the function being accomplished and the form used to accomplish it.

	FUNCTION	FORM
Acts 6:1-7		
Acts 13:1-3		
Acts 19:8		
2 Corinthians 13:12		
1 Timothy 2:8		

Let's Warm Up (10 minutes)

12. What is something you've had a hard time being disciplined about?

Let's Talk (30-50 minutes)

13. Discuss your answers to the "On Your Own" questions. What did you learn about discipline? About form and function? About yourself?

14. Forms can easily be substituted for their functions. For example, going to church becomes an end unto itself, rather than an opportunity to meet with other believers and worship God. What other forms have you seen substituted for their functions?

15. a. Has anyone ever tried to force a particular form on you? Explain.

    b. How did you react?

16. The following statements reflect people's different preferences for how they like life to go. Circle the number that represents where you usually fall on the continuum in each case. When sharing your responses with the group, remember that preferences aren't right or wrong; they're just aspects of our personalities, like whether we prefer chocolate or vanilla.

1	2	3	4	5	6	7	8	9	10
I view change as uncomfortable and disorienting								I view change as challenging but exciting	

1	2	3	4	5	6	7	8	9	10
I try to excel at the traditional ways of doing things								I'm always imagining new ways of doing things	

1	2	3	4	5	6	7	8	9	10
My ideas and attitudes tend to be established and consistent								My ideas and attitudes are evolving	

17. a. What similarities and differences do you observe among members of your group in the ways you've answered question 5?

b. How do you think your preferences in question 5 influence the way you respond to the forms of spiritual disciplines?

18. Jesus confronted the Pharisees about substituting form for function and being disciplined about the wrong things. When the Pharisees

saw that the disciples weren't obeying some of their rules, they came to Jesus to complain. Read Mark 7:5-13. Which functions had the Pharisees confused with forms?

The original function of the ceremonial washing of hands was not physical health. Nobody knew about germs in those days. In fact, nobody had running water, and water was scarce, so dirty water was often reused for the ceremonial washing of hands and dishes.

The function of handwashing was to symbolize cleansing oneself from the spiritual defilement out in the world when one sat down to a sacred act like eating meals. "Clean" and "unclean" were spiritual categories meant to teach people the difference between moral purity and impurity. Much of the Old Testament Law used ritual to teach lessons in a "hands-on" way because most people were concrete learners rather than abstract learners. Concrete learners grasp abstract concepts like moral purity or justice or truth when they have a chance to do something physical with the concept.

So handwashing was not the point; learning the value of inner purity was the point.

The tradition of "Corban" had evolved from the Old Testament practice of offering freewill gifts to the temple. The function of this practice was to express gratitude or devotion to God. At first people simply gave gifts. Then a tradition arose that they could designate a portion of their wealth as a gift to the temple, but retain the use of that wealth until they died. (We do something similar with living trusts to get around death taxes.) This system allowed people to have their cake and eat it, too: use their wealth for themselves and also to win points with God. Eventually, people began designating most of their wealth as a gift to the temple so that they would technically have no money left with which to support aging parents. They could live comfortably without appearing to break the command to honor their parents.

61

19. What do you think Jesus meant when He said the Pharisees had let go of God's commands and replaced them with tradition?

20. What are some forms that you find easy to substitute for God's commands when it comes to your spiritual life?
    ☐ I don't really participate in many common spiritual forms or feel the pressure to do so.
    ☐ Going to church. It often becomes a habit to attend church and I fail to really worship God.
    ☐ Fellowship. It's easy to just enjoy being together for fun without building each other up or actively loving each other.
    ☐ Prayer. I believe I should pray and often do it just to say I did. But I don't have a sense of cultivating an intimate relationship with God when I pray.
    ☐ Tithing and giving money to the church. I often do this because it's expected of me, rather than out of generosity and a commitment to furthering God's purposes in the world.
    ☐ Coming to this group. I have a good time spending time with everyone, and it's easy to let this become a social event.
    ☐ Volunteering my time. I often give my time to charitable organizations to assuage my guilt or because I have trouble saying no, rather than because I feel called to use my gifts to minister to others.
    ☐ Other (please explain):

Let's Act (15-30 minutes)
21. Jesus' response to the Pharisees is scathing. How can you avoid succumbing to legalistic traditions as the Pharisees did, so that you can pursue the true functions of the spiritual life?

22. What are some of the disciplines you practice as a group? Are there any others you'd like to practice?

23. a. Are there any disciplines in your group where the form has out-lasted the function?

    b. What are some guidelines you can use to see if this has happened?

24. How does understanding form and function help you live a disci-plined life under grace?

GROUP WORSHIP   (15-30 minutes)

25. Design your own worship experience based on what you've learned from this lesson.

26. Spend time in prayer committing your group to God and asking Him to keep you aware of the functions behind the forms and dis-ciplines you practice. Pray that He would show you any areas where you've succumbed to following tradition rather than His commands.

Let's Listen to God (15 minutes)
Read aloud the three commitments about listening to God on pages 51-52.

63

27. What do you sense the Holy Spirit is communicating to your group about the following areas?

☐ Your worship and relationship with God

☐ Your relationships with each other

☐ Your relationships with those outside this group

Take a moment to close this conversation in prayer.

Leader:
Before closing this week's lesson, turn to page 66 and assign one or two Scripture passages from question 2 to each person. Each group member should be prepared to share at your next meeting what their passages teach about the purpose of pain and suffering.

6.

TRANSFORMED THROUGH SUFFERING

Much of our activity these days is nothing more than a
cheap anesthetic to deaden the pain of an empty life. I
have tried and I cannot find, either in Scripture or history,
a strong-willed individual whom God used greatly until
He allowed them to be hurt deeply.

—Chuck Swindoll

OVERVIEW

Pain is part of life. People suffer. And pain is often unfair and inexplicable. Explaining why suffering exists is a challenge all religions face.

Some believers claim God wants only prosperity and health for His children and that illness and suffering are not part of His will. But the Bible tells many stories of the suffering of godly people. Suffering seems to have been the norm for God's people throughout history.

In this lesson, we will define suffering, examine our responses to God during times of suffering, and identify areas in which we are experiencing pain. Your goal will be to determine how best to respond to suffering in your own life.

So, what's the big deal?

As God's people, it seems as though we should be exempt from pain. Is it cruel of God to use suffering to transform us into Christ's image?

1. How would you describe pain to someone who didn't know what it was?

2. What are some of the reasons we suffer? Pick the passages assigned to you at the end of session 5 and spend some time thinking about why suffering exists and what it teaches us. Be prepared to share what you learn with the rest of the group.

- ▶ Romans 5:3-4
- ▶ Romans 8:17-18
- ▶ 2 Corinthians 4:17
- ▶ 2 Corinthians 12:7-10
- ▶ Philippians 1:12-14
- ▶ Philippians 4:11-14
- ▶ 2 Thessalonians 1:4-7

- ▶ Hebrews 2:9-10
- ▶ Hebrews 12:11
- ▶ James 1:3-4
- ▶ 1 Peter 2:19
- ▶ 1 Peter 4:12-13
- ▶ 1 Peter 5:9

3. Do you think God feels pain? Explain.

4. How do you usually respond to God when you're in pain?

5. The Psalms are full of examples of suffering. Asaph wrote Psalm 77 out of his distress and offers us an example of how we can approach God with our pain. Read Psalm 77. This psalm is divided into four parts and provides a good example for dealing with pain.

a. How did Asaph express his pain in verses 1-3?

b. In verses 4-9?

c. In verses 10-15?

d. In verses 16-20?

6. What emotions does Asaph express in this psalm?

7. What words would you use to describe how Asaph approached God with his pain?

8. Do you think this psalm is focused more on God or on Asaph's pain? Why do you think so?

9. Is there an area in your life where you're currently experiencing pain or suffering? If so, what is it?

For Additional Study
Does God feel pain? If so, is it the kind of pain we feel? There are many questions about God when it comes to pain. What do each of the following verses teach you about God's response to pain?

▶ Genesis 6:6   ▶ Acts 1:3
▶ Isaiah 53:3,11   ▶ Acts 2:24
▶ John 12:27   ▶ 1 Peter 2:23

 GROUP DISCOVERY   **(50-90 minutes)**

Let's Warm Up (10 minutes)
10. What was your first experience with death when you were a child?

Let's Talk (30-50 minutes)
11. Discuss your answers to the "On Your Own" questions. What did you learn about how you deal with suffering? About your attitudes toward God?

12. Share what you learned about the purposes for suffering from the passages assigned to you at the end of session 5. What are some of the most common reasons for pain and suffering found in the Bible?

13. Have you found these reasons to be true in your own life? If not, can you discern other reasons why you suffered?

14. When you can't see the reason for your suffering, how does that affect how you feel about it?
    □ I get angry. I want to know why I'm in pain.
    □ I trust that God has a purpose for my suffering and that I'll know it eventually.
    □ I feel cynical. Suffering is just part of life and there's never any really good reason for it.
    □ I get anxious. I want to see what God is doing with my pain—is He stretching me or punishing me?
    □ I turn to God for comfort, praying that He'll teach me through my doubt.
    □ I feel scared. What if God doesn't have a purpose for my pain and it's all just a cruel joke?
    □ Other (please explain):

15. Paul experienced his share of suffering. In the beginning of
    2 Corinthians, he explains some of the results of his suffering. As
    you read the following passage from *The Message*, underline the
    words Paul used to describe his suffering.

> All praise to the God and Father of our Master, Jesus the
> Messiah! Father of all mercy! God of all healing counsel!
> He comes alongside us when we go through hard times, and
> before you know it, he brings us alongside someone else
> who is going through hard times so that we can be there for
> that person just as God was there for us. We have plenty of
> hard times that come from following the Messiah, but no
> more so than the good times of his healing comfort—we get
> a full measure of that, too.
>
> When we suffer for Jesus, it works out for your healing
> and salvation. If we are treated well, given a helping hand
> and encouraging word, that also works to your benefit,
> spurring you on, face forward, unflinching. Your hard times
> are also our hard times. When we see that you're just as
> willing to endure the hard times as to enjoy the good times,
> we know you're going to make it, no doubt about it.
>
> We don't want you in the dark, friends, about how hard
> it was when all this came down on us in Asia province. It
> was so bad we didn't think we were going to make it. We
> felt like we'd been sent to death row, that it was all over for
> us. As it turned out, it was the best thing that could have
> happened. Instead of trusting in our own strength or wits to
> get out of it, we were forced to trust God totally—not a bad
> idea since he's the God who raises the dead! And he did it,
> rescued us from certain doom. *And* he'll do it again, rescu-
> ing us as many times as we need rescuing. You and your
> prayers are part of the rescue operation—I don't want you
> in the dark about that either. I can see your faces even now,
> lifted in praise for God's deliverance of us, a rescue in which
> your prayers played such a crucial part.
>
> Now that the worst is over, we're pleased we can report
> that we've come out of this with conscience and faith
> intact, and can face the world—and even more impor-

tantly, face you with our heads held high. But it wasn't by
any fancy footwork on our part. It was God who kept us
focused on him, uncompromised.
(2 Corinthians 1:3-12, MSG)

16. What are some of the results of suffering that Paul describes?

17. Paul says God came alongside him during his suffering. How has
God come alongside you during pain?
☐ He's given me an inner sense of peace.
☐ He's provided supportive people to love and encourage me.
☐ I don't remember feeling God's presence during pain.
☐ While reading the Bible, passages have jumped out at me that
gave me comfort.
☐ He's answered specific prayers about my situation.
☐ Other (please explain):

18. a. Describe a time of suffering where you came through it and
were changed in the process.

b. Do you think you would have learned as much without the
pain? Why, or why not?

After a long battle with leukemia, Marsha's son died. Throughout the struggle, Marsha kept hanging on to God for strength. Two years after her son's death, Marsha was able to look back and see that she was a much stronger, more compassionate person than she had been before her son's illness.

Her friend Carolyn thinks God willed that Marsha's son would get sick and die so that Marsha would grow in her faith. Marsha's husband, Dave, thinks Carolyn's view is sick; he can't imagine God killing their son just to teach Marsha something. Dave resents the effort to find a neat, tidy explanation for the tragedy and is trying to be simply grateful that God brought something good out of the mess.

19. Do you agree with Carolyn, Dave, or neither? Explain.

Let's Act (15-30 minutes)

20. What kind of support would you want from this group while suffering?

21. Does knowing some of the reasons for pain and suffering make it easier for you to understand and accept them? Explain.

GROUP WORSHIP (15-30 minutes)

22. Design your own worship experience based on what you've learned from this lesson.

23. If your group is so inclined, sing an appropriate chorus or hymn.

24. Divide into pairs and talk about areas where you're experiencing pain and suffering. Spend some time praying for each other and

asking God to come alongside you in your pain. Thank Him that there is a reason for suffering and ask Him to make you aware of anything He wants to teach you. Commit to pray for each other during the week.

Let's Listen to God (15 minutes)
Read aloud the three commitments on pages 51-52 about listening to God.

25. What do you sense the Holy Spirit is communicating to your group about the following areas?

☐ Your worship and relationship with God

☐ Your relationships with each other

☐ Your relationships with those outside this group

Take a moment to close this conversation in prayer.

7.

TRANSFORMED WITHIN A COMMUNITY SETTING

If one part suffers, every part suffers with it; if one part is
honored, every part rejoices with it.

—1 Corinthians 12:26

OVERVIEW

The world is a collection of many different communities: countries, cities, towns, religions, political groups, churches, schools, families, and so on. We're all members of communities—some we choose to join, like this group, and others we are part of by where we live or where we were born.

Any community in which we actively participate has the power to help shape who we are. However, the biblical writers envisioned a unique kind of community that is essential to spiritual transformation. While it's possible to grow on our own, a community of this kind offers the Holy Spirit access to our hearts in ways that would otherwise be closed to Him. In the "On Your Own" portion of this session, you'll look at the "one anothers" of the New Testament to learn what the biblical writers expect of a spiritual community. Then in your group meeting, you'll consider several obstacles that can hinder such a community from functioning. Your goals will be to understand how community can help your spiritual growth and what barriers can keep you from experiencing true community.

So, what's the big deal?

Living in an individualistic society, we tend to view spiritual growth as an individual process. But the New Testament shows that community is essential for becoming like Christ. However, growth in a community setting requires honesty and vulnerability. How can we overcome our desire to go it alone and our aversion to letting others see our areas of weakness?

ON YOUR OWN (30-60 minutes)

1. The dictionary defines community as "a body of people living in one place or district or country and considered as a whole; a group with common interests or origins; fellowship, being alike in some way." From these definitions, what different communities do you belong to?

2. In what ways do these communities shape who you are?

3. The New Testament writers used the word *ekklesia*, "those who are called out," to describe groups of believers who functioned as a tightly knit community. God called them out of their ethnic, business, and social communities to be family to each other. As they were transformed in this community setting, God then sent them back to their original communities so that they might draw others to God. What enabled these communities to transform their members?

The New Testament is full of commands about how a community of believers should function. Read each of the verses below and put into your own words what you think it means.

"A new command I [Jesus] give you: Love one another. As I have loved you, so you must love one another." (John 13:34)

Therefore let us stop passing judgment on one another. Instead, make up your mind not to put any stumbling block or obstacle in your brother's way. (Romans 14:13)

Accept one another, then, just as Christ accepted you, in order to bring praise to God. (Romans 15:7)

Be completely humble and gentle; be patient, bearing with one another in love. (Ephesians 4:2)

Be kind and compassionate to one another, forgiving each other, just as in Christ God forgave you. (Ephesians 4:32)

Therefore encourage one another and build each other up, just as in fact you are doing. (1 Thessalonians 5:11)

4. How would each of these influences or behaviors help make you more like Christ?

☐ a community that loves as Jesus loved

☐ a community that doesn't judge or set up obstacles

☐ a community that accepts you as Christ does

☐ a community that bears with you gently and patiently

☐ a community where people are kind, compassionate, and forgiving

☐ a community where people encourage you

5. Have you ever experienced this kind of love, acceptance, et cetera? If so, how did that experience affect you?

6. Obviously, if you were going to be part of such a community, then you would have to learn to treat others like this habitually. Which of these attitudes and/or behaviors is hard for you to practice consistently?

7. When you contemplate a community of this kind, what do you feel?
   - [ ] Longing to experience something like that
   - [ ] Sadness that I've never had that
   - [ ] Discomfort at the thought of letting people that close
   - [ ] Anger that nobody treats me that way
   - [ ] Gratitude for the community I have
   - [ ] Relief to have some picture of what "community" means
   - [ ] Cynicism because it's easy to talk about love and acceptance, but quite another thing to practice it
   - [ ] Annoyance because acceptance is fine, but people also need confrontation
   - [ ] Other (please explain):

8. Would you like your small group to practice these "one anothers"? Why, or why not?

9. Look ahead to question 8 in "Let's Act." Be thinking of ways you can affirm the people in your group.

For Additional Study
Paul describes the community of believers as one body. Read 1 Corinthians 12:12-32. What do you learn about how members of a community are related to one another?

Let's Warm Up (10 minutes)

10. Name one person who made you feel loved when you were a child. How did they do that? (If you can't think of anyone, it's okay to say you can't. How did that affect you?)

Let's Talk (20-30 minutes)

11. Discuss the questions in the "On Your Own" section. What did you learn about community? About yourself?

12. Where would you fit on the scale below?

1	2	3	4	5	6	7	8	9	10
I prefer to be alone								I prefer to be with others	

13. What more often makes you change or grow—a personal conviction or someone else bringing something to your attention?

14. What is the one thing from the "one anothers" in the "On Your Own" section that you most long for in a community?

15. Although many of us long for the kind of community that accepts, forgives, and encourages, we sometimes avoid the opportunity to get involved. In your experience what gets in the way? Check as many as apply.

☐ Time
☐ Fear
☐ Family
☐ Work
☐ Lack of priority
☐ Other (please explain):

16. What could you do to overcome these obstacles?

Let's Act (35-60 minutes)

Fear is one of the most common reasons we avoid community. The thought of being vulnerable and honest with others is more than a little frightening. What if they dislike or don't accept me after hearing my thoughts? What if I'm the only one who's ever struggled with this? What if they don't keep what I say in this group?

How can you as a group encourage and build up one another? One way is an exercise like the following:

17. Take some time to go around the room and affirm each person present. Begin with a volunteer. Let everyone share what you admire about that person or what he or she has added to the group. You may tell that person what he or she brings to your mind or the feelings he or she evokes. You can simply list words that describe that person or describe an object that represents that person to you. The important thing is to let the person know what you appreciate about him or her.

When everyone has said something about the first volunteer, ask for another. Continue until everyone has had feedback.

If your time is limited, you could decide that each person will receive affirmations from four people instead of from the whole group. It's important that everyone receive affirmations from at least a few people, rather than that a few people receive from everyone.

Alternatively, you could plan that before the next meeting you will each write down one thing you have gained from each person in the group. Write each of your affirmations on a separate card so that you can give them to each person when you meet again.

18. While the above exercise affirms the good we see in each other, it doesn't address the fear most of us harbor that, if people knew our shortcomings, they wouldn't be so willing to embrace us. How could your group overcome such a foundational obstacle to community?

19. What could your group do to become the kind of community that the New Testament prescribes?

GROUP WORSHIP (15-30 minutes)

20. Design your own worship time based on what you learned from this session.

21. Sing an appropriate chorus or hymn if you desire.

22. Spend time praying together as a group that God would transform your group into a tightly knit community. Pray that He would show you ways to build each other up and encourage one another in your spiritual growth.

8.

LET'S PERSONALIZE CHRISTLIKENESS

OVERVIEW

In this session and the next, you will review and apply the lessons you have learned in sessions 2–7. In this session you will focus on personal lessons and applications, while session 9 will focus on group applications. As you prepare for your group meeting, remember to pray frequently. Some inventory work will help you select the one key truth from sessions 2–7 that is most urgent for you personally. Then your group will help you think through appropriate action steps and life changes you can pursue. Your goal will be to settle on one key truth and the action you can take to build it into your life.

So what's the big deal?
It's better to be obedient in just one area about which God is convicting you than to fill up a workbook full of good intentions about several truths, none of which you obey or profit from.

ON YOUR OWN   (30-60 minutes)

1. What changes are you beginning to see in your relationship with God as a result of this study?

☐ Any mistakes you are avoiding?

☐ Any attitudes you are changing?

☐ Any areas of new freedom in Christ?

☐ Any changes in the way you view God?

☐ Any new ways you feel or things you do when you spend time with God?

2. Review what you have studied and discussed in sessions 2 through 7. Try to state one or two truths that stand out to you as most important in each session. For example, for session 7 you might write, "A loving, patient, encouraging community is essential for a person who wants to become like Christ."

☐ Session 2

☐ Session 3

☐ Session 4

☐ Session 5

☐ Session 6

☐ Session 7

3. You may have repeated yourself in question 2, circling around the
   same one or two truths that jump out at you from every session. If
   so, it may be that the Holy Spirit has put His finger on an area of
   focus. Take a moment to pray about your list of truths. Put a star
   beside the one that you think is most important for you to address
   in the near future. Or, combine several of the truths into one, and
   state it below. (Don't get sidetracked trying to summarize all of
   your truths into one overarching thesis. The point is to pick one
   limited idea that you can reasonably grasp and focus on.)

4. How has this truth affected your thinking and behavior so far?

5. How do you think the Holy Spirit would like this truth to affect your life—your thoughts, feelings, and actions?

Be prepared to share your key truth and its effects with your group. They will help you formulate a plan for integrating that truth into your life and acting on it. They will also help keep you accountable to the degree that you allow them to do so. You're not in this alone!

 GROUP DISCOVERY (50-90 minutes)

Let's Warm Up (10 minutes)
6. What is one thing you have gained from this group during the past seven sessions? What is one thing for which you are grateful?

Let's Talk (45-80 minutes)
Plan your time so that you have at least five minutes for each person to share his or her truth and receive help in formulating a plan of action. Ten minutes each would be even better, but that might require going overtime. Be sure that no one is shortchanged of this opportunity for help.

7. Read to your group your key truth, how it has affected you so far, and how you think the Spirit would like it to affect you. Then, with help from the group, come up with a plan for integrating your key truth into your life. Ask yourselves the following questions as you help each other plan your strategies:

☐ Is the key truth clear?
☐ What results or outcomes would you like to see from this plan of action?
☐ Are the action steps specific and realistic?
☐ Not all action steps in the spiritual realm are quantifiable. For example, praying for thirty minutes a day is quantifiable, but genuinely opening your heart to God in prayer is not. How will you know if the changes you are pursuing are really happening?

Here is an example of a plan that is practical, specific, measurable, and clear:

The key function of the spiritual life that I have been missing is a moment-by-moment setting my mind on what the Spirit desires. That has weakened my ability to respond to suffering as Jesus would have done. First Peter 1:13, where it talks about preparing my mind for action and setting my hope on future grace, keeps coming to mind. So I'm going to copy that verse onto a card. For the next two weeks, I'm going to devote five minutes before work and five minutes after work to reading it over and over, thinking about what it means for me that day to set my hope on Christ. I'm also going to try to remind myself of this thought throughout my day by posting the verse over my desk. One friend from this group is going to call me every other evening to encourage me to keep at this, and to hear what I've learned from the experience.

Write your plan here (you may continue on the top of the next page):

8. List anything you have committed to do for someone else in your group:

9. Use this space to list the other group members' key truths (you will need these to do your personal preparation for session 9):

| ❤ | **GROUP WORSHIP** | **(15-30 minutes)** |

10. Design and implement your own time of worship. Be sure to include prayer about your key truth and your plans for applying it.

9.

LET'S GROW TOGETHER IN CHRISTLIKENESS

OVERVIEW

The work you do this session will be similar to session 8 in that you will review and apply the lessons you have learned in sessions 2–7. In this session your goal is to come up with an application for your whole group, whereas last time the focus was on personal application.

Planning group applications requires hard work. You will be thinking in areas that may be different from anything you have tried before. Six areas have been selected to help you evaluate your group's progress.

So what's the big deal?
If you persevere, you will achieve powerful results. You will be growing not just as individuals but also as a community of believers.

ON YOUR OWN   (30-60 minutes)

Throughout the course of these studies, you have had experiences that contributed to your sense of community. Take a few minutes to assess the progress and contributions your group has made in spiritual sensitivity, worship dynamics, relational intimacy, functional interdependence, mission focus, and sphere of influence. This assessment procedure will help you evaluate your group's progress and help you plan for your future relationships.

1. **Ability to listen to the Holy Spirit.** In a group with high sensitivity to the Spirit, you will observe unity and peace created by the Spirit, or you will observe people allowing the Spirit to disrupt their complacency and challenge their assumptions. On a scale of 1 (low) to 5 (high), how would you rate your group's sensitivity, receptivity, and responsiveness to the Holy Spirit's leadership?

1	2	3	4	5
low				high

2. **Worship dynamics.** God is the central focus in worship. Recall your worship times in the preceding sessions. In a group with "rich" worship dynamics you can expect to find a sense of God's majestic presence with you, variety, and everyone participating and contributing. On a scale of 1 (poor) to 5 (rich), how would you assess the overall quality of your group's worship experience?

1	2	3	4	5
poor				rich

3. **Relational intimacy.** The Bible is full of relational terms such as love, forgiveness, acceptance, reconciliation, and bearing one another's burdens. As you experience these conditions, your group will grow in relational intimacy. Evidences of "deep" intimacy are high levels of trust, vulnerability, transparency, honesty, and mutual commitment. On a scale of 1 (shallow) to 5 (deep), how would you assess your group's level of intimacy?

1	2	3	4	5
shallow				deep

4. **Functional interdependence.** The church is the body of Christ, a living organism with many members. Your small group functions like a system in that body, working interdependently with other systems and their members. Not only that, each member of your group is gifted to perform specific tasks that contribute to the overall internal functions of your group. On a scale of 1 (harsh, grating) to 5 (sweet, synchronized), how well are the members of

your community working together toward a common task, and
how harmoniously is your community working alongside others?

1	2	3	4	5
harsh, grating				sweet, synchronized

5. **Mission focus.** Christian communities can easily become self-absorbed. This happens when they turn a deaf ear or a blind eye to what's on God's heart and, instead, focus their attention on themselves. The result is a diminished heart for the world that God loves and gave His Son to die for. God uses groups to reach into every nook and cranny of the world. On a scale of 1 (self-absorbed) to 5 (other-focused), how motivated is your group to looking beyond itself and fulfilling God's mission to reach the world?

1	2	3	4	5
self-absorbed				other-focused

6. **Sphere of influence.** God's mission is global in scope, including all kinds of people—rich and poor, men and women, young and old, Black, White, Hispanic, Asian, et cetera. Although we are to be open to new ministry opportunities, God often calls a community to minister within its specific sphere of influence. This sphere sets limits that sharpen your focus. On a scale of 1 (confused, non-existent) to 5 (sharply focused), how clear is it to your community who God has called you to minister to?

1	2	3	4	5
confused				focused

7. Review all the truths and life applications that you and your fellow group members identified last time. What is the one truth from these studies that you feel is most relevant for your whole group collectively? (This may be different from what is most significant to you personally.)

Let's Warm Up (10 minutes)

8. In what one way has this group helped you become more like Christ?

Let's Talk (30-45 minutes)

9. Share progress on personal applications from the last session. Are you helping each other follow through on your commitments? How so? Thank God for the progress He has already made among you.

10. Remember, community building is a process. Some members of your group may desire greater intimacy, and some may feel threatened by the intimacy already achieved. God is still at work in your group in the six areas you assessed on pages 90-91. He is molding you into a vehicle fit for Him to use however He wills. Review the six areas of assessment and compare answers as a group. Pay special attention to major differences in your evaluations. How do you account for these differences?

11. Discuss what each of you thinks is the one significant truth most relevant to your group (identified in question 7). Try to come to a group consensus of the one truth and its implications for your group. To reach that consensus, here are some helpful hints:
    ☐ Begin with prayer, asking God to clarify your thinking.
    ☐ List the truth from each individual on a chart or white board.
    ☐ Look for duplications and related themes. Consolidate and combine where possible.

☐ Build consensus on one truth. Sometimes related thoughts can be combined to better reflect the overall truth but beware of stringing ideas together into a broad, complicated conglomeration.

☐ Don't worry about a perfect statement. Blend the ideas of each person in the group to arrive at the consensus position. (Designate someone in the group who has an aptitude with words to edit for clarity and length. Take the statement home to polish it up, if necessary.)

12. Write your group truth here.

13. Next you will plan how to integrate this truth into your group life, much as you did for each individual group member last time. Your first step will be prayer. Take five minutes to ask God to lead you in this process. You might ask, "Lord, how would you like our group to put this truth into practice?" or "God, what would you like our community to become?" Listen quietly. As you have thoughts or impressions, either make mental notes or jot them down.

14. Write three headings on newsprint or a white board: God, One Another, Others. Under the first heading, list ways in which this truth should affect your group's relationship with God. Under the second heading, list ways in which this truth should affect your relationships with each other, and so on.

God	One Another	Others

15. Now brainstorm a fourth list: things you can do to put this truth into practice in your group. Call out ideas without evaluating or criticizing any of them.

16. After five or ten minutes, stop and sort the ideas into short-range steps and long-range steps. Edit them so that each one is a realistic, doable action that lends itself to accountability. Who will do what, by when, where, and for/with whom? Weed out any impractical ideas. Try to come up with at least one short-range and one long-range step that meet these standards.
    □ What is it?
    □ Who will do what?
    □ By when?
    □ Where?
    □ For/with whom?

    a. Short-range steps

    b. Long-range steps

Because learning to implement this truth as a community is so important, you should commit yourselves to take as many sessions as needed to work out your group application. Place a higher priority on implementing your plan rather than moving on to another study.

17. Design and implement your own time of worship. Be sure to include prayer about your key truth and your plans for applying it. Also, thank God for what you have received from this study. Celebrate your time together, both your past and your future.

If you set out to identify the core elements of the Christian life, what would your list include?

After ten years of Bible study involving thousands of believers from countries all around the world, The Navigators' SCRIPTURAL ROOTS OF LIFE team saw a few basic themes emerge over and over again:

WORSHIP
Worship: Honoring God in All of Life
(ISBN: 1-57683-007-1; 9 sessions; 96 pages)

COMMUNITY
Relationships: Resolving Conflict and Building Community
(ISBN: 1-57683-023-3; 9 sessions; 96 pages)

INTIMACY WITH GOD
Intimacy: Pursuing Intimacy with God
(ISBN: 1-57683-010-1; 9 sessions; 96 pages)

BECOMING LIKE CHRIST
Christlikeness: Committing Ourselves to be Changed by God
(ISBN: 1-57683-006-3; 9 sessions; 96 pages)

THE TRINITY
Restoration: Discovering How God Meets Our Deepest Needs
(ISBN: 1-57683-009-8; 9 sessions; 96 pages)

THE UNSEEN WORLD
Warfare: Discovering the Reality of the Unseen World
(ISBN: 1-57683-026-8; 9 sessions; 96 pages)

SHARING THE FAITH
Outreach: Sharing the Real Gospel with the World
(ISBN: 1-57683-012-8; 9 sessions; 96 pages)

WORK
Work: Serving God on the Job
(ISBN: 1-57683-024-1; 9 sessions; 96 pages)

Designed to foster close-knit community within your group, the FOUNDATIONS FOR CHRISTIAN LIVING series is a great way to grow strong in faith, life, and love for God. Available at your local Christian bookstore. Or call 1-800-366-7788 to order.

NAVPRESS
BRINGING TRUTH TO LIFE